Fragrance Of A New Dawn

Easter Sunrise One-Act
By Louis Merryman

C.S.S. Publishing Co.
Lima, Ohio

FRAGRANCE OF A NEW DAWN

9120 / ISBN 978-1-55673-287-4   PRINTED IN U.S.A.

Dedicated to Kathy Pocsics, fellow script writer, who edited the manuscript, Pastor Paul Radford, my producer, and the Life '89 Players, who made it all happen.

Suggested Order of Service

Prelude

Call to Worship: Come! Come let us rejoice in the good news of this Easter morning. Christ Jesus is risen. Death could not hold him. He has risen from the grave! Alleluia!

Opening Hymn: Jesus Christ is Risen Today

Invocation: O God our Father, we praise your name this glorious resurrection morning for your son, Jesus Christ, who by his death and resurrection redeemed us for eternal life. We now ask your acceptance of our praise and worship this early morning. Help us to overcome our doubts as you did with the saints of the early church that we might fully understand the majesty and the miracle of Easter. Through Jesus Christ our Lord. Amen.

Doxology:

Prayer of Confession: Like Thomas, we do not believe until we have seen. Like Moses, we would let Aaron do it. Like Martha, we would be working and not listening to your words of truth. Forgive us for our lack of belief, our refusal to accept responsibility, and our selective deafness. Strengthen our belief, open our eyes, and let us hear you, our Savior and our Lord.

Assurance of Pardon: John 6:37

The Lord's Prayer:

Hymn: Low in the Grave He Lay

The Nicene Creed: *(Optional)*

Special Music:

Scripture Lessons: Old Testament: Isaiah 53
New Testament: John 20

Morning Prayers:

Offerings:

Introduction to the Drama: Luke 23:33-56

The Drama: "Fragrance Of A New Dawn"

Hymn: I Serve a Risen Savior

Benediction: Go and tell them! He is risen! He is risen indeed!

Fragrance Of A New Dawn
SCENE ONE

Cast:
Mary 1 — Mother of James and Joseph, Mid 40s
Salome — Mother of James and John, Mid 40s
Ruth — Widow of Nain, 50s
Mary 2 — Martha's sister, 40s
Martha — Mary 2's sister, 40s
Judith — Jairus' wife, 30s
Phoebe — Wife of a Roman Centurion, early 30s
Mary 3 — Mary Magdalene, attractive woman, in her late 20s
Angel 1 — Warrior Angel
Angel 2 — Warrior Angel
Jesus — Risen, 33

Note:
An attempt has been made to adhere to the customs of Israel in A.D. 29. Sandals are not worn indoors and the "shawl" headcovering is worn on the head outdoors only. When traveling in cold or windy weather, the face is covered.

Setting:
We are in the spacious entry to the home of Zebedee. The entry to the courtyard and the rest of the house is at stage right. The door to the street is at left. A table laden with basins of water, towels, three large shoulder bags, small pieces of cloth to protect the spice vials, and at center right, vials of perfumes and spices. At upstage center and center left are wooden benches.

At Rise:

SALOME sits on the upstage center bench, weeping. She is dressed in a bright green robe with a white headdress. MARY 1 kneels in front of RUTH washing her feet. MARY 1 is dressed in a dull brown robe, RUTH in a dark blue robe. Both have matching headdress. RUTH carries a small shoulder bag. It is 4 a.m. on the first Easter Sunday.

RUTH: *(Appreciative)* It feels good to have these old feet washed by you, Mary. The walk from Nain was terrible! The cold cut right to the bone. The wind was strong, too. It seemed like all nature was joining me in my grief over Jesus' death.

MARY 1: Many people, Ruth, are mourning the death of the master. If it wasn't against the law, I would scream a mourning wail that all of Jerusalem would hear.

RUTH: The **wailing woman** in the marketplace was doing just that. The middle of the night and she's howling at the top of her lungs. She woke up everyone who lived near the marketplace. *(Chuckles)* It was quite a sight. The neighbors were screaming at her and at each other. Her escort was yelling back. The wailing woman just sat there in the middle of the night mourning her lost love.

MARY 1: *(Hesitatingly)* Was the woman Jewish . . . or Gentile?

RUTH: *(Thoughtfully)* I . . . I . . . think she was Gentile, Salome.

SALOME: *(Stops sobbing, sits up, loudly, with malice)* It's her . . . that Roman wench. She was here. I told her I didn't want her or her spices. I sent her packing, back to Capernaum. She apparently didn't get too far. *(Buries face in hands, sobs)*

RUTH: *(Quietly, to MARY 1)* Mary, you know the wailing woman?

MARY 1: Yes, she's a proselyte from Capernaum. Married to a very generous centurion. She was here earlier.

RUTH: *(Impressed)* My!

MARY 1: It really upset Salome. She doesn't believe proselytes can ever become true daughters of Abraham. And **we watched** the Romans kill Jesus. Phoebe — that's the wailing woman's name — is a Roman. Right now she's not welcome anywhere near this house.

RUTH: *(Haughty)* Well, I hope she goes back to Capernaum, too. I hate Romans. I was almost arrested by a Roman patrol tonight.

MARY 1: Really!

RUTH: They stopped me just outside of Nain. When I told them I was bringing spices for the Master's body, they got upset. "Wearing black," they said, "to mourn an executed criminal is a crime." They let me go only after they saw my robe was dark blue.

MARY 1: They can stop us from wearing mourning clothes and wailing, but they can't stop us from grieving in our hearts. *(Smiles)* Salome and I are defying the Romans. I am wearing a dull brown. It's the closest thing I have to mourning colors. Salome is wearing a bright color, just the opposite of mourning clothes.

RUTH: Wonderful!

MARY 1: *(Admiring)* Phoebe was really smart. Her traveling robe was as black as night, but the robe underneath was pure white. I'll bet she was covered up and not telling anyone whom she was mourning.

RUTH: You're right. No one ever mentioned the name of the deceased. *(Sarcastic)* And you sound like a Roman-lover.

MARY 1: Jesus said we should love our enemies, even the Romans. I try to do that. It's difficult, but I try. Phoebe, even if she is a Roman, mourns Jesus as much as we do. She's figured a way to get around the law about no mourning clothing and no wailing. I admire that. *(Pause)* Enough of this talk about Romans. After Mary Magdalene gets here, we'll be going to the tomb. What spice did you bring?

RUTH: *(Caring)* I brought some Rue Two. *(Takes small vial from shoulder bag)*

MARY 1: *(Stops washing, dries hands)* Thank you! *(Receives vial)* Smells . . . *(Pulls stopper)* delightful.

RUTH: It's not much.

MARY 1: It's very special. Friends have been bringing spices, perfumes, and ointments ever since sabbath ended. Magdalene, Salome, and I are going to take all of them to the tomb at first light. Would you like to join us? *(Stands)*

RUTH: I'd love to. My son, even at this sad time, needs to spend time with his wife. Who knows, I might even become a grandmother again!

MARY 1: You're a grandmother?

RUTH: I'm a grandmother. My daughter-in-law had a little boy!

MARY 1: *(Stands, hugs RUTH)* That's wonderful! You must be the happiest woman in Nain.

RUTH: *(Thrilled)* And I have Jesus to thank for it all.

MARY 1: What do you mean?

RUTH: *(Remembering)* Three years ago, within the space of three months, both my husband and son died. It was during my son's funeral procession that I met Jesus. I was weeping bitter tears. I had no relatives to care for me. I would be destitute and alone. Jesus took compassion on me and raised my son from the dead.

MARY 1: How wonderful!

RUTH: That was the start of many good things.

MARY 1: *(Beaming)* Your son got married. Now you're a grandmother!

RUTH: *(Joyously)* We named him James.

MARY 1: *(Happily)* One of my sons is named James. We must celebrate. *(Kneels)* We'll go to the kitchen. *(Picks up towels and basin, rises)* and fix a snack. *(Pauses, smiles)* After we eat, would you like to rest before we go to the tomb?

RUTH: I . . . Yes, I would. Thank you.

MARY 1: Salome, I'm going to find a place for Ruth to lie down.

SALOME: *(Does not move)* Fine.

MARY 1: *(Happy)* We'll add your spice to the collection. *(puts vial and basin on table, keeps towels)* Thank you again.

RUTH: It's the least I could do.

MARY 1: *(Sadly)* I know. He did so much for us. *(Begins to exit right)* Ohh . . . I'm getting morbid. Let's get you settled down before I become a wailing woman.

(MARY 1 and RUTH exit right)

(SOUND — KNOCKING ON DOOR)

MARY 1: *(Continued)* *(Offstage)* Can you get the door, Salome?

SALOME: *(rises, slightly irritated)* Of course. *(To herself)* They won't let me mourn in peace. *(wipes tears from her eyes as she goes to the door. Opens door)*

MARTHA: *(Dressed in dull blue, enters in a rush. A fast talker, MARTHA allows neither SALOME nor MARY 2 to say anything until she finishes talking)* Shalom! *(Hugs SALOME)* May the peace of the Lord be upon this house!

SALOME: Martha! May the . . .

MARTHA: *(Breaks embrace, goes quickly to table, begins to examine towels for cleanliness by looking at and sniffing them)* We heard about Jesus' death and the way they just . . . just shoved his body in the tomb before the sabbath started. I don't think he would have liked that. We were **thrilled** when we heard . . .

(MARY 2, dressed in bright yellow, enters, hugs SALOME twice as MARTHA continues talking)

MARTHA: *(continued)*. . . that you were going to the tomb and properly prepare Jesus' body. We'd go, too, except that Lazarus needs us. Poor man, he went into a state of shock when he heard Jesus was to be crucified. They were such good friends. Lazarus just sits on a chair now and stares into space. A neighbor agreed to look after him so we could deliver these spices. *(Deep sniff of a towel)* You really must watch your servants, Salome. Whoever prepared this towel left out the perfume. And this one . . . *(Another sniff)* smells like the whole bottle was emptied on it. *(Looks at SALOME)* May I use this towel to wash Mary's feet?

SALOME: *(Who has not been listening)* Excuse me, what did you say?

MARTHA: May I use this towel when I wash my sister Mary's feet?

SALOME: I'll wash.

MARTHA: Nonsense! You've probably been up all night answering the door and collecting spices. *(Takes basin and towel to left bench)* Every time we visit, you tell me to make myself at home. Well, I'm doing it. Come Mary, I'll wash your feet.

SALOME: *(with MARY 2 joins MARTHA, forthrightly)* And I'll wash yours. I'm the hostess!

MARTHA: *(Kneels, sadly)* I've washed Jesus' feet . . . *(MARY 2 sits down)* so many times. I won't be able . . . *(Brings towel to her eyes)*

SALOME: Let me do that! *(Drops to her knees beside MARTHA. MARTHA reluctantly lets SALOME begin the footwashing of MARY 2)* Please sit on the bench, Martha.

(MARTHA sits on the upstage end of the bench, MARY 2 is on downstage end.)

MARY 2: *(Graciously)* You're a gracious hostess, Salome. The walk was very tiring. *(Slight pause)* The last time Jesus was with us, I bathed his feet with a whole vial of Sweetnardia No. 3. It made the entire room smell so sweet! Then I dried his feet with my hair. I don't know why I did it. I just did!

(SALOME finishes with MARY 2's feet, starts MARTHA's)

15

MARTHA: *(Most unloving)* Judas, that traitor, nearly had a fit. He called Mary all sorts of names. Said we could have sold the spikenard Mary had used on Jesus' feet and given the money to the poor. He didn't care about the poor. He wanted to put the money in **poor** Judas' pocket.

MARY 2: Jesus knew he was going to die. He said, it was meant that I should have saved this perfume, this Sweetnardia, for the day of his burial.

SALOME: *(Finishes MARTHA's footwashing)* He raised others from the dead. Is there anyone who could do the same for him?

MARTHA: *(Stands, goes to table)* What about your sons, James and John?

SALOME: Typical men. Like the rest of the disciples, they're in hiding. They're afraid of the priests, the Romans, and their own shadows. My own Zebedee has gone fishing. He's afraid he might be arrested. If the soldiers come, they'll only have us to arrest.

MARY 2: *(Stands, terrified)* You don't suppose . . .

SALOME: *(Stands, reassuring)* Zebedee checked with some of his friends at the temple before he left. We women won't be bothered. And the priests are more afraid of Jesus than anyone else.

MARY 2: Why are the priests afraid of Jesus? He's dead.

SALOME: The priests and Romans are afraid the disciples will steal Jesus' body and claim he's alive. They've covered the tomb with a heavy stone. There's an armed guard, too. *(Smiles)* They certainly don't know the disciples. They've been in hiding for three nights.

MARY 2: *(Goes to left, wondering)* I think Jesus said he'd be back.

MARTHA: At the resurrection, when we are all raised.

MARY 2: *(Turns, defensively)* That's what we said to him just before he raised Lazarus from the dead. Jesus said he was the resurrection and the life! *(Agressively)* Maybe what Jesus needs is someone to stand before his tomb, pray, and then say **Jesus, come forth!** Maybe I'll go to the tomb with you and . . .

SALOME: *(Aghast, scolding)* Mary, that's ridiculous! If the soldiers don't kill you, God will, for your blasphemy.

MARY 2: Someone needs to do something!

MARTHA: *(Firmly)* Someone is! Salome, Mary, and Mary Magdalene are going to finish preparing Jesus' body. We shall all see him again at the resurrection.

SALOME: *(Goes to MARY 2, comforting)* I'm sorry I spoke harshly to you. We each mourn in different ways. Would you like to go to the tomb with us?

MARY 2: Will you be long?

SALOME: The more hands, the faster the work will be done.

MARY 2: *(Happily)* Let's do it, Martha!

MARTHA: But Lazarus needs . . .

MARY 2: Jesus needs us this one last time.

MARTHA: Well, all right!

MARY 2: We'll go.

MARTHA: *(Smiling)* Then help me sort these spices. They're in one big pile and the scents are starting to fight each other. Phew! *(Makes face, holds nose)*

(SOUND — KNOCK ON DOOR)

MARTHA: *(Moves toward door)* I'll get it!

SALOME: *(Moves to door)* No, I'll get it, Martha. If it's Mary Magdalene, she's on time for the first time in her life. *(Opens door)*

JUDITH: *(Dressed in a bright blue robe with a white headdress, a shoulder bag over one shoulder, enters, joyously)* Shalom. May the blessings of the Lord be upon your house.

SALOME: *(Excited)* Judith! And may the peace of God be with you!

(SALOME hugs JUDITH. MARY 2 and MARTHA rush over and welcome JUDITH with hugs and squeals. SALOME leads JUDITH to bench at left)

SALOME: *(Continued)* You look wonderful. Did you just come all the way from Capernaum?

JUDITH: Oh, no, we came down last week for Passover. Jairus, young Mary, and I are staying with friends. We are still trying to get over Jesus' death. *(Sits on bench)*

MARTHA: *(Gets basin and towel from table)* It's been awful! *(Goes to upstage end of bench)*

SALOME: Everyone's afraid. My Zebedee went fishing as soon as sabbath was over. He always goes fishing when he has problems or is avoiding the Romans.

JUDITH: Jairus went to the temple to pray at dawn yesterday. Then he walked around Jerusalem for hours. And on the sabbath? He's never done that before.

MARTHA: *(Kneels)* Jesus' death has upset everyone. *(Holds up towel)* Let me honor you, Judith.

SALOME: *(Irritated)* Martha! What are you doing? I'm the hostess!

MARTHA: I'm trying to wash Judith's tired and dusty feet!

JUDITH: I've only come from six blocks away!

MARTHA: From the looks of your feet, those are the six dustiest blocks in all of Judea.

SALOME: *(walks around bench to downstage of MARTHA, kneels)* Martha, I insist. This is my job!

MARTHA: I just want to help . . . and besides, you've been up all night. *(Grasps JUDITH's right foot)*

SALOME: This is my house, and I will wash my honored guest's feet! *(Grasps JUDITH's left foot)*

MARY 2: *(Standing behind JUDITH, grasps JUDITH's shoulders as she begins to fall backward off bench. JUDITH half-turns and grasps MARY 2's waist for support. MARY 2, tries to keep from laughing as she scolds)* Martha! Salome! You're embarrassing Judith by your childish behavior. I suggest you cleave her in half with a large sword. Then you'll both have a foot to wash.

JUDITH: *(Wincing)* I have a better idea.

SALOME: I would hope so.

JUDITH: *(Decisively)* I will decide who cares for my hot and dusty feet.

MARTHA: Good idea!

SALOME: Brilliant. I just know you'll make a wise decision.

JUDITH: I choose Mary!

MARTHA: *(Surprised, drops foot)* Mary! She's so inexperienced.

SALOME: (Happy, MARTHA was not chosen) A decision worthy of one of Solomon's race. *(Releases foot. stands)* Mary, the honors are all yours.

MARY 2: *(Releasing JUDITH)* But it's your home.

SALOME: And Judith's decision.

MARY 2: *(Appreciative)* Thank you. *(Goes to front of bench)*

MARTHA: *(Goes to table)* I'll sort the spices.

SALOME: I'll help. *(Joins MARTHA at table)*

MARY 2: *(Kneels)* And I'll render the hospitality of the house of Zebedee. *(Begins to wash)*

JUDITH: *(Enjoys)* Delightful.

MARTHA: There's a really good selection of spices and perfumes here. Aloe . . . in abundance. *(Opens vial, sniffs)* Oh, so sweet!

SALOME: Frankincense! What a scent. *(Whiffs)* A rhapsody of aroma.

MARTHA: Jesus' mother told me a wise man from the East gave him frankincense when he was a baby. *(Holds up vial)* And myrrh, too. *(Opens, sniffs)* O, what a lovely fragrance! When I die you can cover me in myrrh!

SALOME: *(Whiffs a fragrance, pleased)* This is Zebedee's favorite. It's made from the blossoms of the baytree. Zebedee gives me anything I want when I snuggle up close to him, smile sweetly, whisper in his ear, and let him get a whiff of baytree blossoms. It reminds him of our honeymoon. Ummm! Baytree blossoms!

MARY 2: Is there any spikenard?

MARTHA: *(Looks)* I don't see any.

SALOME: *(Holds up vial, playfully)* How about some Rue Two, instead?

MARTHA: *(Critical)* Rue Two? At least it's not Rue One. Rue One has no scent at all.

SALOME: One of the poor widows brought it. It was the best she could do.

JUDITH: Then it is a very rich gift indeed. But I prefer the balm from Beth Shan, myself.

MARTHA: It's here. *(Holds up medium sized vial)* There are several here.

JUDITH: It appears that we have all found our favorites except for Mary.

MARY 2: *(Finishes footwash, disappointed)* Spikenard was Jesus' favorite. One woman poured some over his head. I poured an entire vial over his feet. It was Sweetnardia No. 3, the finest and most costly of all the spikenards. I had hoped . . .

JUDITH: *(Happily)* The wife of our synagogue's most generous benefactor is bringing several vials of Sweetnardia No. 3. A runner came from Capernaum earlier this evening with the news.

MARY 2: *(Stands, joyously)* Praise God! Three vials. That's worth a king's ransom!

JUDITH: She should have arrived by now. Her husband provided an armed escort.

MARY 1: *(Enters from right)* Ruth is resting. *(Sees JUDITH and MARY 2)* Judith! Mary! *(Runs to MARY 2, hugs her)*

JUDITH: *(Happily)* Mary! *(Hugs MARY 1)* You're looking good!

MARY 1: You too!

MARTHA: *(Hugs MARY 1, happy)* Shalom.

JUDITH: We are delivering spices. I almost forgot. Here's mine. *(Hands vial to MARTHA, to SALOME)* This is balm from Beth Shan, my personal favorite.

MARY 1: *(Happy remembering)* I'm an old-fashioned girl. I love calamus. Brings back, ummm, nice memories.

SALOME: We have two vials of it.

JUDITH: When Phoebe gets here, Mary will have her favorite fragrance.

MARY 1: *(Ashamed)* Phoebe?

JUDITH: One of our proselytes. Her husband is most generous to our synagogue.

SALOME: *(Sarcastically)* Trying to buy his way into heaven, no doubt.

JUDITH: *(Correctingly)* Oh, no. Jesus once said that he had greater faith than any son of Abraham.

MARTHA: Jesus said that?

JUDITH: What is more amazing is that the man is a centurion.

SALOME: *(Visibly upset)* Your centurion's fellow soldiers killed Jesus.

MARY 1: *(Forthrightly)* Only because the sons of Abraham are forbidden to execute anyone. The sons of Abraham **had the chance** to release Jesus. They didn't.

JUDITH: Ladies, please! Jairus, the centurion's family and I, share a common bond thanks to the Master. Jesus brought our daughter back from the dead. He did the same for the centurion's servant.

MARY 2: I can understand that. We thought we would never see Lazarus again.

MARTHA: Jesus raised him from the dead, too. *(Slight pause)* If I remember the story correctly, the centurion sent some men from the synagogue to see Jesus because he **respected** our custom of no contact with gentiles.

JUDITH: The centurion recognized the Master's authority over death even from a distance. *(Pauses)* But what has all this talk about Phoebe's husband to do with the Sweetnardia Phoebe is bringing?

SALOME: *(Quietly, stares at table)* She was here.

MARY 2: What?

MARY 1: Phoebe was here earlier. We chased her away.

MARY 2: Why? She . . .

SALOME: *(Loudly, defensively)* She's a filthy Roman. The filthy Romans killed Jesus.

JUDITH: Not Phoebe.

SALOME: *(Hysterically)* Roman hands held the hammers that drove the nails into his flesh. Roman arms pushed and pulled the cross upright. Roman dice determined who would win his robe. He wore a crown of thorns fashioned by a Roman officer. Roman iron pierced his side. *(Catches her breath)* **Romans,** dirty filthy Romans killed him! *(Screams next words)* I was there. I watched the Romans kill Jesus. He's dead. It's all over. *(Deflated)* Jesus said it himself. It's finished.

JUDITH: *(Goes to SALOME, gently)* We understand. But Phoebe is mourning Jesus as much as we are.

MARTHA: *(Arm around SALOME)* Would you like to lie down?

SALOME: Thank you, no. I'll be okay. We need to pack these vials into these shoulder bags. Will you help me?

JUDITH: Of course. *(JUDITH wraps vials in cloth, puts them in bag.)*

(MARTHA and SALOME help put the vials in the bags.)

MARY 1: Jesus forgave his executioners. We all heard him. I believe we should forgive Phoebe of her misfortune to have been born a Roman and accept her gift.

MARY 2: Spikenard was Jesus' favorite fragrance. If he could, he'd forgive Phoebe and bless her for her thoughtfulness.

MARTHA: If we don't use the spikenard on Jesus, it will be used on some dead Roman.

JUDITH: This is your home, Salome. The decision to let Phoebe into this entryway is yours.

SALOME: Well, it's Jesus' favorite, and why should it be wasted on a . . . *(Snarled)* **Roman.**

MARY 1: *(Smiling)* I'll go get her. I hope she's still in the marketplace. *(Goes to door)*

JUDITH: I'll join you. *(Joins MARY 1, both exit)*

SALOME: I made a fool of myself.

MARY 2: You should have seen me when Lazarus died. I was beside myself in grief. I was angry at everyone, even the Master.

MARTHA: We knew that if Jesus had come sooner Lazarus would not have died, but it didn't happen that way.

SALOME: I had hoped that Jesus would do something about the Romans. *(Hateful, clenches fists)* Romans!

MARTHA: None of us like them, Salome, but, I do like Phoebe. I just wish she had been born Jewish.

MARY 2: I think they're coming! *(Turns to door, ditto MARTHA and SALOME. JUDITH, MARY 1 and a reluctant PHOEBE, dressed in a black traveling cape and white robe with a complementing gold necklace, enter. PHOEBE has a large black shoulder bag)*

JUDITH: Come on!

PHOEBE: *(Hesitation)* Are you sure it's all right?

MARY 1: *(Reassuring)* It's all right. We came and got you, didn't we?

PHOEBE: Yes, but this whole trip has been one terrible thing after another. *(JUDITH, PHOEBE and MARY 1 stop behind bench)*

MARY 2: Judith told us you were bringing Sweetnardia No. 3. Jesus loved that particular fragrance.

SALOME: Judith vouched for you as a follower of the Master. I'm sorry I chased you away earlier. Can you forgive me for my behavior?

PHOEBE: *(Gratefully)* Of course. *(PHOEBE takes the first of three tall slim vials from her shoulder bag and passes it to JUDITH, who passes it to MARY 2, who passes it to MARTHA, who puts it on the table. Vials two and three are passed the same way.)*

MARY 2: *(Excited)* Oh, Sweetnardia No. 3!

MARTHA: *(Impressed)* These must have cost a small fortune.

SALOME: *(Impressed)* In some lands, only kings can use this.

PHOEBE: Jesus deserves it. He'll always be a king to me. At one time, I thought my husband believed the same thing. *(Hand to face, weeps)*

JUDITH: I don't understand. No one is more devoted to Jesus than your husband!

PHOEBE: *(Apologetically)* He said many strange things before I left. He said I was a foolish woman for coming here. He said I wouldn't find a body and if I did, it would be the body of a charlatan.

MARTHA: *(Appalled)* Jesus was a charlatan?

MARY 1: No!

SALOME: *(Angry)* Get out of my house. Go back to Capernaum! *(Moves menacingly toward PHOEBE)*

PHOEBE: *(Backing to door, pleading)* He didn't mean it. Please let me explain.

SALOME: Just leave! *(JUDITH, MARY 1 and MARY 2 form a line in front of PHOEBE. MARTHA follows SALOME)*

JUDITH: *(Loudly)* Salome, please!

SALOME: I want her out of my house.

PHOEBE: *(Defiantly)* I'll go. But I wish you'd let me explain!

MARY 2: We can keep the Sweetnardia, can't we?

MARTHA: Absolutely!

SALOME: *(Points to door)* Out! *(PHOEBE exits)*

SALOME: *(Continued)* Thank you Lord! She's gone! *(The five women gather around the spice table and complete the job of filling the shoulder bags — MARTHA, SALOME, JUDITH, MARY 1 and MARY 2)*

JUDITH: I think she needed to explain herself. Her husband would never have said anything like that.

SALOME: He's a Roman, isn't he?

MARY 2: She meant well. These are fine gifts. *(Holds up vial)*

(SOUND — LOUD POUNDING ON DOOR)

MARTHA: That's probably Mary Magadalene. I'll let her in.

SALOME: Thank you, Martha. *(SALOME, JUDITH, MARY 1 and MARY 2 continue to wrap the vials. MARTHA opens the door. They look up and watch MARY 3, dressed in flaming red, drag reluctant PHOEBE to the front of the left bench. They have not removed their sandals)*

MARY 3: *(Demanding)* What have you done to this poor woman? She's a nervous wreck! You owe her an apology and a chance to explain some things.

SALOME: *(Defensively)* Her husband called Jesus a charlatan.

MARY 3: I know. I heard.

MARTHA: Were you listening at the door?

MARY 3: How could I not hear? All of Jerusalem heard! *(Pause, demanding)* Has anyone shown Phoebe the hospitality of this house?

JUDITH: *(Apologetically)* No.

MARY 3: Phoebe has come all the way from Capernaum. She's tired and dusty. Her feet hurt. Who's going to wash her feet? Who's going to fix her some food and drink?

SALOME: She's a Roman!

MARY 3: She's a proselyte, a daughter of Abraham by choice, not by birth. After the way she's been treated by us and the way the high priests treated Jesus, I'm surprised she gave you the Sweetnardia.

MARTHA: What will the neighbors think?

MARY 3: What would Jesus think?

SALOME: With all respect to the dead, Mary, Jesus probably couldn't care less now. At least the neighbors are alive.

PHOEBE: My husband doesn't think so.

MARY 1: *(Aghast)* Your husband thinks the neighbors are dead?

PHOEBE: Oh, no. *(Hesitantly)* He thinks Jesus is alive. *(The OTHER WOMEN are shocked at this statement)*

PHOEBE: *(Continued)* As a matter of fact, he expects to have dinner with Jesus later this week.

MARY 3: *(Gently)* Your husband's words are very confusing. First he calls the Master a charlatan and then he expects to have dinner with a dead man.

PHOEBE: *(Settles onto bench, fatigued)* I fear my husband has gone quite mad.

MARY 3: *(Quickly goes to table, gets towel, returns, kneels before PHOEBE, removes PHOEBE's sandals)* I really want to hear you out. You've traveled a long distance with the most expensive gifts. The least we can do is listen and show you some hospitality.

(SALOME glares at MARY 3 and PHOEBE)

PHOEBE: *(To MARY 3, humbly)* You don't have to wash my feet, Mary.

MARY 3: *(Factually)* The Master drove seven demons from me. He forgave me for sins too dark to mention. I don't care what the neighbors think. Jesus would approve. *(Starts footwashing)*

PHOEBE: That is refreshing. This is the first time I have been able to sit down and relax since the dispatch rider brought the news of Jesus' trial and execution.

MARY 1: Please tell us exactly what your husband said.

PHOEBE: Are you sure you want to hear this?

MARY 3: Yes.

PHOEBE: *(Confidently)* You must promise never to tell any of this to his fellow centurions. They would think he had gone crazy.

SALOME: *(Curious)* We won't tell.

MARTHA: Men don't believe anything we tell them anyway. Your words are safe with us.

PHOEBE: My husband shut himself in his study after the dispatch rider left. I wandered from room to room trying to think of something I could do for Jesus. I finally decided to come to Jerusalem and bring some Sweetnardia for his body.

MARY 2: Thank you!

PHOEBE: My husband was studying the scriptures when I entered his study. I asked him for an armed escort for my journey.

MARTHA: He agreed?

PHOEBE: He laughed at me.

SALOME: You poor woman!

PHOEBE: He said the trip was a waste of time. If I found a body it would be the body of a . . . *(Stands, defiantly)* I told him in no uncertain terms that Jesus was no charlatan. He was a holy man and a prophet and I would not tolerate such talk!

SALOME: Good for you!

PHOEBE: I don't know what got into me. I've never talked that way to my husband before.

JUDITH: Every so often they need to hear from us.

PHOEBE: He took me in his great arms and hugged me. "I agree with you," he said. "Jesus is more than a holy man and a prophet. He is the fulfillment of prophecies, the Messiah, and he is **the** Holy One of Israel. He's just as alive as you or I."

JUDITH: He has gone mad!

MARY 3: *(Rises, arm around PHOEBE)* You don't have to continue.

MARTHA: But we'd love to hear it.

MARY 2: Martha!

JUDITH: Talking it out helps. Please continue. *(MARY 3 releases PHOEBE)*

PHOEBE: He knew he had shocked me. Then he said, "When my servant, Tobias, was dying, I asked Jairus to go to Jesus and ask for Tobias' healing. As you know, I am a man of authority, a centurion. When I speak, I speak for the emperor, the senate and the people of Rome. Legions march, battles are fought, kingdoms fall, kingdoms rise. Tobias had been with me on many battlefields. When I saw death on his face, I knew there was nothing I could do. Not I, nor the emperor, nor the senate, nor all the legions of Rome. With a word, Jesus stopped death in his tracks. Tobias rose, healthy and smiling. My servant had been restored to me."

MARY 1: *(Thrilled)* We know **that** story. What **else** did your husband say?

PHOEBE: "When death meets me, I will die. But when death meets Jesus, death will meet the one he **cannot** kill. The master is alive!"

SALOME: Men just can't handle these things calmly. They start acting strangely and leave all the work to the women.

MARTHA: Your husband should go fishing or take some long walks like Jairus.

MARY 3: *(Kneels, gathers basin and towels)* Alive! I pray it were true.

MARY 1: Is there more?

PHOEBE: *(Sits on bench)* Unfortunately, yes.

JUDITH: It's our duty to hear you out. Please continue.

PHOEBE: Are you sure? *(ALL nod yes)*

PHOEBE: *(Excited)* He started waving his arms and walking around the room. He looked at me and smiled the biggest smile. "You want to do something special for Jesus?" I nodded my head, yes. "I know just the thing! Shortly after Jairus' daughter was brought back from the dead, Jesus told them to give her something to eat." *(Really excited)* "He's probably hungry!" *(Waves arms)* "Take the Sweetnardia to Jerusalem. Find Jesus! Pour the perfume over his head and feet. Invite him to dinner! Here — next week." *(drops to bench, wails)* I'm not here to honor Jesus' body! I'm here to invite him to dinner.

(MARY 3 sits on bench downstage of PHOEBE. SALOME sits on bench upstage of PHOEBE. MARY 2, MARY 1, MARTHA and JUDITH gather behind PHOEBE.)

SALOME: You poor dear.

MARY 3: Your husband is insane.

SALOME: I want you to stay here with us. We'll treat you as an honored guest. We'll put your escorts up in the servants' quarters.

PHOEBE: Thank you.

MARY 1: Would you like to go to the tomb with us?

PHOEBE: *(Smiles)* I'd be honored!

SALOME: *(Stands)* I'll have the servants fix us something to eat before we go. I'll be right back. *(Exits)*

MARTHA: Phoebe can help us pack the spices in the bags. *(MARY 3 and PHOEBE stand)*

MARY 3: After all, she's one of us. *(MARY and PHOEBE embrace)*

JUDITH: A daughter of Abraham.

(BLACKOUT)

END OF SCENE ONE

Fragrance Of A New Dawn
SCENE TWO

Setting:
> The path from Jerusalem enters the area in front of the tomb at downstage right. Other paths enter at upstage right and downstage left. The tomb entrance is at upstage left. The tomb's door, a large round stone is at upstage center. Portions of a red Roman wax seal are on the stone and on the side of the tomb entrance.

Rise:
> The stage is empty. It is dawn, the first Easter Sunday.

> *(MARY 3, SALOME and MARY 2 enter from downstage right. Shawls cover their faces. Each has a shoulder bag filled with spices)*

MARY 3: *(Stops, as does SALOME and MARY 2, center left. Uncovers her face, happily)* And we wondered who was going to roll the stone away for us. Someone's already done it.

MARY 2: *(Uncovers face, thankful)* That's a relief. That thing looks really heavy. *(MARTHA and MARY 1 enter downstage left followed by JUDITH, PHOEBE and RUTH)*

MARY 2: I shall use the Sweetnardia last. Phoebe can help me pour.

PHOEBE: I'd like that. *(ALL group together at center right, faces are uncovered)*

MARY 1: Wonderful!

PHOEBE: It shouldn't be. That's an imperial seal. The penalty for breaking one of those is death.

SALOME: You're acting like a Roman.

JUDITH: She's right. And where are the soldiers guarding the tomb?

RUTH: *(Looks around, afraid)* This place is giving me goosebumps.

MARY 3: There's nothing to be afraid of here. Not a thing.

MARY 1: *(Bravely)* Then let's go in! *(Covers face, starts toward tomb)*

MARY 3: The rest of you better wait here. We'll go inside first and check on the state of the body. *(Covers face, follows MARY 1)*

SALOME: *(Turns to MARY 2, weeps)* I don't know if I can do this. I want to remember him alive, not as a dead body. *(MARY 1 and MARY 3 enter tomb)*

MARTHA: There's something wrong here. When they opened Lazarus' tomb, the stench was terrible. I don't smell death. I smell only the fragrance of a **new** dawn.

MARY 2: *(Sniffs air)* She's right. We used many spices on Lazarus and there was still a horrible smell. It lingered in the air for several hours after the tomb was closed again.

RUTH: *(Looking around, fearful)* I don't like this! My goosebumps are getting goosebumps.

PHOEBE: I'm beginning to wish I had my escort.

MARY 3: *(Inside tomb, hysterical)* Eeeeeeeeeeeeeeeek . . . eeeeeeeeeeeeeeeek . . . eeeeeeeeeeeeeeeek!

(ALL on stage huddle close together, look around fearfully)

MARY 2: What was that?

PHOEBE: Someone screamed!

SALOME: Magdalene! *(SALOME runs toward the tomb entrance followed by the rest of the women. At the entrance SALOME is met by a near hysterical MARY 3, who leads them to center stage. MARY 1 follows, fear etched on her face.)*

MARY 3: (Hysterical) Someone has taken his body. It's not here. Who took it? Who took Jesus' body? *(To PHOEBE, angry)* Did any of your filthy Roman friends do it?

PHOEBE: *(Tearfully, fearfully)* No! No! No Roman would dare break an imperial seal.

MARY 3: *(To herself)* The priests? No, they're afraid of the Romans. The disciples?

SALOME: They're hiding.

MARY 3: *(Angrily)* I know where they are. If they didn't take his body, I'll bet they know who did. *(Runs to downstage right)* I'm going to get Peter. He'll know. He'd better know! *(Desperately)* Someone's got to know! *(Exits)*

SALOME: *(Runs to right, stops)* Mary! Mary! *(Turns to rest of them)* She's gone. We'll never catch her.

MARTHA: *(to MARY 1)* What happened in there?

MARY 1: *(Shaking)* There's no body. He's gone. The only things left are the grave linens.

RUTH: *(Nasty, to PHOEBE)* Can the Roman who ordered the tomb sealed order it unsealed?

PHOEBE: *(Fearfully)* Yes, but . . .

RUTH: I think the Romans took the body. There's no guard. *(Stares at PHOEBE)* How do we know you're not some kind of spy?

PHOEBE: *(Aghast)* Noooo!

SALOME: *(Surprised)* I never thought of that.

MARY 1: *(Defensively)* But Phoebe is so much like one of us.

MARTHA: A good spy would be like that.

MARY 2: Martha!

MARTHA: It's true.

MARY 1: Not Phoebe. She and her husband love our God. She's one of us. Isn't that right, Judith?

JUDITH: *(Hesitantly)* Yes, that's right!

SALOME: I believe you, Judith. But just in case . . . *(To PHOEBE)* we're going to keep our eyes on you. And . . . you can't go into the tomb!

RUTH: Right!

SALOME: *(To Ruth)* Stay here and watch Phoebe while we go in the tomb.

RUTH: Stay here? You stay here. You're the one who wants someone to watch her. I want to go into the tomb.

PHOEBE: Why can't I go into my Lord's tomb?

MARTHA: You may defile it. We don't want to take any chances.

MARY 1: Please try and understand.

PHOEBE: And I thought I was one of . . . *(breaks into tears and runs to the face of the stone where she sinks to her knees and leans against the stone. The others watch her)*

SALOME: Such a scene! I think we can go in without her now.

MARY 1: Follow me. *(MARY 1 leads MARTHA, RUTH, MARY 2, SALOME and JUDITH into the tomb. PHOEBE stands, looks at JUDITH, JUDITH sees her and turns)*

PHOEBE: I thought you were my friend, Judith.

JUDITH: *(Steps toward PHOEBE)* I am.

PHOEBE: Way down deep? Mary washed my feet and made me feel at home. Then she turned against me.

JUDITH: *(Honestly)* It's difficult not to have such feel-ings. *(Hugs PHOEBE, tears, pleads)* Forgive me, please, forgive me. I want to be your friend. I don't care what the neighbors think!

PHOEBE: Thank you. Thank you. *(JUDITH watches in awe as ANGEL 1 and ANGEL 2 enter from upstage right. The angels are dressed in shining white robes, with mirror-surfaced breastplates and great sheathed swords on their backs. Their height, military bearing, and serious looks impress JUDITH)*

JUDITH: *(Nervous)* The Romans didn't move the stone. I'm sure of it.

PHOEBE: *(Happily, breaks hug)* You're sure of it?

JUDITH: *(Frightened)* Very sure.

PHOEBE: You sound like you know who moved the stone. Who moved it?

JUDITH: *(Gulps)* **They** did. *(Kneels)*

PHOEBE: *(Turns, awed)* Who? Who are they? *(Kneels)*

JUDITH: *(Awed)* I think they're angels. *(Turns head to face tomb)* Salome! Mary!

SALOME: *(From tomb)* What now? *(Enters, awed)* Ohooooo. *(Kneels) (MARTHA, MARY 1, MARY 2 and RUTH enter from the tomb and drop to their knees as they see the angels)*

ANGEL 1: *(Gently)* Don't be afraid. We won't hurt you.

ANGEL 2: We know you look for Jesus of Nazareth, who was crucified.

ANGEL 1: He's **not** here! He has risen.

ANGEL 2: As he said he would.

ANGEL 1: Go quickly. Tell his disciples. He's alive and is going before you into Galilee. You'll see him there.

(The ANGELS exit, ALL the women look at each other in awe and wonder at what they have seen and heard. They stand and joyously enjoy the good news: Jesus is alive)

MARY 1: *(Joyously)* Those were his words, "I shall rise on the third day." *(Hugs SALOME)*

SALOME: I remember! I remember!

MARY 2: *(Excited)* "I am the resurrection and the life." *(Hugs MARTHA)* I remember! I understand!

RUTH: He's alive! *(Hugs SALOME and MARY 1)*

JUDITH: Your husband is right. He's alive. *(Hugs PHOEBE) (JESUS enters, downstage right. He is dressed in a white robe with a purple mantle over one shoulder. He wears white sandals)*

SALOME: We must tell the disciples! *(SALOME, followed by MARY 1, RUTH, MARY 2, MARTHA, JUDITH and PHOEBE start toward downstage right. As each woman sees JESUS, she kneels before him. JESUS talks to each in turn, helps them rise, and stand to his stage right)*

JESUS: *(Cheerfully)* Good Morning!

*** THE FOLLOWING LINES ARE SAID TOGETHER ***

SALOME: *(Awe)* Master! *(Kneels)*

MARY 1: *(Awe)* Jesus! *(Kneels)*

RUTH: *(Awe)* Lord! *(Kneels)*

MARY 2 and MARTHA: *(Awe)* Jesus! *(Kneels)*

JUDITH: *(Awe)* Master! *(Kneels)*

PHOEBE: *(Fearful)* Jesus! *(Backs to stone, kneels)*

*** END OF SAID-TOGETHER LINES ***

SALOME: It is you, isn't it?

JESUS: *(Helps SALOME stand)* Yes. I've risen from the dead and am quite alive.

MARY 1: *(Joyously)* You said you would!

JESUS: *(Helps MARY 1 stand)* I want you to tell your sons and the rest of the disciples that I'm alive and well. I will meet them in Galilee.

SALOME: We will, Lord, we will!

JESUS: *(To SALOME)* Give Zebedee my regards. I'll see him soon, too. Perhaps we'll go fishing.

SALOME: I shall! *(SALOME and MARY 1 step to the right, JESUS moves to in front of RUTH)*

RUTH: *(Hides her face)* Forgive me, Lord. I spoke ill of the only one of us who said that you would rise. I'm not worthy to look you in the face.

SALOME: *(Sorrowfully)* We all treated Phoebe badly. We're sorry. Phoebe is one, truly one of us. And her husband is a man of great faith.

MARY 1: He knew you would rise!

JESUS: You're all forgiven. *(To RUTH, helps RUTH rise)* and you shall be a grandmother many more times.

RUTH: *(Ecstatic)* Thank you, Lord! *(Moves to right)*

JESUS: Dear Mary, dear Martha. Don't be frightened. It is indeed your friend, Jesus. *(Helps MARY 2 and MARTHA rise)*

MARY 2: *(Tearfully, examines JESUS' hands)* Did it hurt?

JESUS: It hurt, but only for a while.

MARTHA: Can we help in any way?

JESUS: Thank you, no. I'm fine. I want you to run home and tell Lazarus the good news. Have him meet me in Galilee.

MARY 2: *(Joyously)* I can't wait to get home!

MARTHA: Lazarus will be so surprised! *(Moves with MARY 2 to right)*

JESUS: Judith! *(Helps JUDITH rise)* How is little Mary? And Jairus?

JUDITH: *(Tearful joy)* When I return to them and say "He is risen!" their grief will turn to joy. We will run all the way back to Capernaum.

JESUS: You are a faithful servant, Judith. I look forward to a more lengthy visit with your family when I come to Capernaum.

(JUDITH steps to right)

JESUS: *(Continued) (Gently)* Phoebe.

PHOEBE: *(Turns face into rock)* I'm a Roman, Jesus. My people killed you. My husband said you were alive, but I didn't believe him. I've disgraced him and you. Will you forgive me?

JESUS: *(Kneels)* Of course! I forgave those who crucified me, and I forgive you.

PHOEBE: *(Looks at JESUS)* But why did you have to die? I don't understand.

JESUS: Forgiveness of sin requires a blood-sacrifice.

PHOEBE: Like the one at the temple?

JESUS: Yes, but not any longer. I was the final sacrifice.

PHOEBE: No more sacrifices?

JESUS: My Father requires no more sacrifices.

PHOEBE: *(Points to other ladies)* The sacrifices at the temple were for them. Was your death just for them, or for me, too?

JESUS: I died that all people might be saved. That includes you, Phoebe, and all your fellow Romans.

PHOEBE: *(Stumbling)* My husband said you were the promised Messiah, **the** Holy One of Israel.

JESUS: *(Smiling)* And who do **you** say that I am?

PHOEBE: *(Continued)* You are the Son of God! And my Lord, my Savior. *(takes JESUS' hands, BOTH stand, rejoicing)* and I am so glad to see you alive. Will you join my husband and me for dinner?

JESUS: Please tell your husband that I accept his invitation for dinner and will join both of you for the evening meal on Thursday. *(JESUS turns, holds his hands up as the WOMEN look at him)*

JESUS: *(With joy)* Now go, quickly. Tell my brothers what you have seen and heard. I have risen as I said I would. I will meet them in Galilee!

(BLACKOUT)

END OF THE PLAY